Hungry Spring
&
Ordinary Song

COLLECTED POEMS

(an autobiography of sorts)

Hungry Spring & Ordinary Song

COLLECTED POEMS

(an autobiography of sorts)

PHYLLIS TICKLE

PARACLETE PRESS
BREWSTER, MASSACHUSETTS

2016 First Printing
Hungry Spring and Ordinary Song: Collected Poems
(an autobiography of sorts)

Copyright © 2016 by Tickle, Inc.

ISBN 978-1-61261-788-6

Library of Congress Cataloging-in-Publication Data

Names: Tickle, Phyllis.
Title: Hungry spring and ordinary song : collected poems : an
  autobiography of sorts / Phyllis Tickle.
Description: Brewster, Massachusetts : Paraclete Press, 2015. | Includes
  index.
Identifiers: LCCN 2015037854 | ISBN 9781612617886
Classification: LCC PS3620.I28 A6 2015 | DDC 811/.6—dc23
LC record available at http://lccn.loc.gov/2015037854

10 9 8 7 6 5 4 3 2 1

Published by Paraclete Press
Brewster, Massachusetts
www.paracletepress.com

Printed in the United States of America

CONTENTS

The Liturgical Year in Lucy

THE "WOMAN AT MIDNIGHT" POEMS

Portraits

Other Places of the Heart

THREE
ARS POETICA

FOUR
ENUIGS

FIVE
COMMEMORATIVE

SIX
ENDINGS

A BRIEF INTRODUCTION

I AM NOT A POET, or at least not one as that term is usually applied or technically defined. But over the years of my writing life, I have come upon experiences and events and even perhaps a few epiphanies where the rhythm and the cadence of the thing was as much of its truth and vitality as were the words themselves. To the extent that that phenomenon is poetry, or at least describes it, then what follows is poetry.

Many though certainly not all of the pieces assembled here have appeared from time to time over the years in various and sundry venues; and I have made no attempt to trace their bibliographic history here. What I have done over the last few months is to organize the disparate parts and moments, perceptions and givens, of my years into some kind of coherence or whole. The result, almost by default, is "an autobiography of sorts." And thus my subtitle. But I have also attempted to add from place to place a few comments that I hope will enrich the whole by making some of the attendant circumstances clearer.

As for the organization of the pieces themselves, I have looked back over my own years, as well as the poetry that has arisen from them, and come to believe that some areas of life are so central as to be core to what we are. Certainly for me, gender has been an informing and perhaps even the centralizing factor. By gender, of course, I do not mean sexuality, though, thank God, that is certainly here and part of the whole. I mean rather that I think we come into life with a gendered predisposition not only to roles and physical abilities, but also to sensibilities and sensitivities and proclivities for bonding and alliances, joys and vulnerabilities. Mine, as recorded here, are those of a woman, as is my conviction that such has informed and shaded everything else I have known or lived.

The second most formative and informing part of experience and its interpretation, it seems to me, is place itself: the places where we stop awhile, where we plant ourselves, where we give ourselves to an environ and in which we give ourselves to others who are likewise stopping there. Like most older post-twentieth-century Americans, my husband Sam and I not only lived our years in several places, but also lived our free or wandering time in others. Each of those places seems to me to have been part of the pastiche of sensibilities and experiences that make any life story, and certainly have made mine.

As for the other categories, I trust they will be equally useful, if not quite so fraught with need for explanation or annotation. I hope even that some of them will be "fun" or a source of droll humor, if nothing else, for I have enjoyed using words sometimes to parry with life. Otherwise, the whole might have proved too much. I have enjoyed as well the opportunity from time to time to commemorate events and people that, almost without my playing scribe, were themselves poetry.

And last of all, sometimes some of us are blessed with a creative or writing partner whose affections and perceptions are not only sympathetic to one's own, but also invigorating and instructive. Years ago I was so blessed by coming to know and write with Margaret Bartlum Ingraham. We have done a good deal of work together, some small bits of which are included here. Thus, when a piece is marked as "A Natalie Bartlum Poem," it is of our work together, for my middle name is "Natalie," and hers, obviously, "Bartlum." I hope I am correct in saying that we both are, and have been, grateful for this sharing over these years.

As for the rest, I shall leave the "Endings" section to say what may yet be left to say. Certainly, as I conclude my eighty-plus years of life, for the grace of endings I am perhaps most grateful of all.

Phyllis Tickle
The Feast of St. Bartholomew, 2015

Hungry Spring
&
Ordinary Song

COLLECTED POEMS

(an autobiography of sorts)

To reduce my being to a tiny book
And, in my lap, to hold it there—
To separate the me from what I am
And know what other men can share—
This is the pinnacle of art,
The juncture of living and the dream.

ONE

SONGS OF GENDER

THE HYMNS OF HYMEN

I
Hymen Yet Unbroken

I am (I know it) much too weak.
Dear God, ashamed I own it!
Heaven help me then retreat
To some sweet, static state
Removed from this love's bittersweet.
To leave untouched what I can not complete
And let another, being stronger, drink the sweet.

No! Pray God rather
That I be no more too weak
To fill the need I first awoke,
Like the broken rush of a dammed-up creek.
To bear with him love's sorrow
And dare with him love's dare.

II
Hymen Still Unspoken

You tell me sadly that it can not be,
That if there were some magic key,
Some sweet pattern for expression,
Poets would have found it long ago.
And thrown their pens to a sanguine flow.

You smile and gently kiss my hair,
Laughing silently at my futile, barren show
That words, chafing within me, should plague me so.

But whatever you, chiding, say of me,
Whatever you say has never been, can never be,
This much through all my soul I know—
I must ease the pain from so intense a glow
And pray its labored song may free
Some other kindred soul who, like me,
Is drunk on love's long infinity.

III
Hymen Broken

Sometimes it sweeps over me in icy waves of quiet,
Flooding all being in one pristine burst of light
Beyond the scope of thought.
It swells in visions bold with holy light
That you who lie beside me in the silent, sleeping night,
That you whose nocturnal breath caresses hair and cheek alike,
That you, living, are my life;
That by some sacred tie beyond my breadth of thought,
My soul is tied to yours in a welding blaze
We two alone did not ignite;
And miracle breaks on miracle in resounding waves of light
That, walking through the wood of years,
I have left the night.

IV
Hymen Spoken

I often think, when I peruse the distant world of childhood,
That I had surely loved you then.
For love like this must be-is-more by far
Than formless, deathless end.
It must have sucked upon eternity before
It walked the lonely shores of time
And seen the dawn of plan rise up, smoking,
From infinite, almighty Mind.
It must have found in Heaven's holy lanes
The symphony it was born to sing
And held it natal hymn uncrushed—
Though strangely, strangely dimmed—
In adolescent memory.
Now let that chorus glorious re-echo to its boundless home
'Til you and I no longer sound its mournful tones alone, alone.

In Perpetuum

A boy dug a hole beside the sea
Where waves rolled froth and blast
To lace the sand with urgency.
The sea came in at last.
The hole, which caught it fast,
Wailed, "Fill up all of me."
Then there was only sea,
And thus it is with you and me.

Perspective

From my attic window
The tree tops in the storm
Show silver like the stria
On my belly.

Interstate 40

An October Passion Poem

The autumn vinegar
Of a startled skunk
Roughs my nose,
Tempts me
To try the air
Again
And then once more.
The cave-sharp scent
That returned hunters to their lairs
Stirs history.
To lie down and give perfume!
I dream of ramps with exits
In the long hours home to you.

After an Illness

I come to my body unwillingly,
Like a woman of the night.
Some circumstance of poetry
Has lured me back.
So long away, so late returned
I wonder most
Who knew your touch
While I was thus delayed.

Anniversary Song

Written as a gift for our twenty-fifth anniversary

When you and I were young then,
Children in the town,
When you and I were young then
Under the spreading yarrow,
You in your knickers
And I in my gown,
Playing at house in a mountain town,
Playing as children do,
Under the bending yarrow.
Its boughs were green,
But its needles were blue,
And love was dreams
Under the singing yarrow.

The nights are long in a mountain town,
And all for the love of ease,
We laid us down,
You in your knickers
And I in my gown,
Under the spreading yarrow.
Its needles were soft,
Its branches were blue,
And we slept the whole Spring through,
Under the singing boughs
Of gleaming mother yarrow.

Under the murmuring yarrow tree,
Under the needled clouds and brown-wood cones,
Behind the hill and along the rill
Of the rushing river stream,
We played at house, as children will,
Under the wind-crowned yarrow.

You left your knickers and I my gown,
And under the kindly yarrow
You laid me down,
Laid me down to dream
Of children then
Born beneath a yarrow tree.
But above the lullaby of sky,
We heard the brave elk's cry
And now are gone
From under the murmuring yarrow.

Snow sleeps deep upon the arms
Of aging mountain trees,
But soft are the boughs, and blue the light,
In the woodland halls
Of the cloud-wrapped yarrows.
Warm is the air and warm the earth
Under the spreading limbs
Of the silvered yarrows.
You in your knickers and I in my gown
Are caught in the winter's wind,
Are lulled by the pine trees' songs,
While down below, along the rill
And under the midnight hill,
None can remember, none recall,
The April day
We slipped away,
You in your kickers and I in my gown,
To play at house,
As children will in a mountain town,
Under the blue-green boughs
Of kindly mother yarrow.

The Laments

I

My unfilled hours settle into days,
And grief wearies into sadness.
Even love cannot survive
The violence of such passing.

II

This child was a thought in the mind
Who, though he died,
Can have no ending.

III

When the redness of my pain
Has died away to brown,
I arrange myself like foliage
To feign a full bouquet.

IV

The body heals, but the heart—
Schooled and taught—still hesitates
Reluctant to accept
Another and unending pain.

Of the many experiences singularly defined and imposed by gender, perhaps none is so wrenchingly painful or so isolating for a woman as miscarriage. Even the most loving partner cannot enter into the nature of such pain. It was for me an ongoing and frequent part of life, for we lost more infants before birth than I can even name now, their loss being tempered only by the ultimate loss of our infant son in 1971.

Medusa Quietly Screaming

For Wade: 29 May – 11 June, 1971

There was such an easiness in your going,
Such a stilling peace for us once they said,
   "He's gone."

It filled up all our days that came and went
Until our friends began to say,
   "Won't you come to dinner?
   "Attend this play?
   "See ballet?

    "Take for your sorrow some cliché of
   'God will provide' or
   'Life must go on'?"

And so it is, my son,
That the work of your burying
Has begun.

Menarche

Lovely little thing
That was wont, in former days,
To go tripping like a melody,
I mourn the pathos that has changed you,
The pathos of the opera.
Yet for a woman, I suppose,
The opera is more fitting.

For Rebecca on a Sunday Morning

Your father laid you into me with pain;
I still can hear the groan he gave.
And those low moans I made
Before I gave you back to him?
From a joy so like his pain
That I am ashamed
When I remember now.

To My Daughters

I raped myself and found me good,
Warm in all the smells and folds
That are our mother parts,
And tough as well
Beneath a paunch
That's baby-sprung.

For Each Daughter on Their Wedding Day

I

He's a strong man,
This boy who claims your hand—
Silly exercise, since he's long since won.
Take him to your bed now
And make of him a son
Who's as blond and firm as he;
And in your doing,
Buy eternity for me.

II

Because I have missed you,
Say quickly the vows that will ferry you.
Once we were nearest friends
Before your birth and growing
Washed you out from me,
Away from this side of knowing.
But nearer friends than that can be
Once you've crossed back again
Through him to me.

III

The girl to woman grown
Forgets old joys in sorrow sown;
Forgets with an unseemly haste
The art of being chaste;
Forgets the skills of shame
And finds new freedom in a name.

IV

Once we were nearest friends,
Before your birth and growing
Washed you out from me,
Away from this side of knowing.
But dearer friends than that, my girl,
Can be,
Once you've crossed back again
Through him to me,
Back to this side of knowing.

Morning Song

Suckle a baby
Suckle a man
Take a lover
And guide his hand.
Suckle a baby
Suckle a man
Lift the route
And lift him in.
Suckle a baby
Suckle a man
Drain his quiver
And let them out.
Suckle a baby
Suckle a man
Nurse the child
And hold the man.
Suckle a baby
Suckle a man
Be the woman
Meek and mild
Suckle a baby
Make the man.

Upon Receiving, after Her Death, My Mother's Earrings in the Mail

The Chinese scroll
Is a lattice of gold
Lacquered in green
And hung on the screen
Of mulattoed black
Where she always stored her preen.

Stroked like a harp
Fashioned from oak
Whose music is smoke,
Incensed like her and sharp
(Though she can't re-appear),
The lattice still sings to my brain
In a nursery refrain
Of abandoned evenings I feared.

O sacred smoke,
Giving out gall like the oak,
A ghost in the dancing shoes of seems,
Resurrect the dragon dream.
Don, if you dare, the ancient gold.
This time you will find I can hold.
This time it is I who am souled.

Sometimes it is easy to forget the dark side of motherhood ... or of dependent childhood with even the most adored and adoring mother. I shall never forget the day when, as a fully adult wife and mother, I opened this packet, found the earrings there, and suddenly was awash in the memories of anxiety and temporary abandonment their presence always presaged for me as a child.

The women of the Abrahamic tradition have certainly been made much of over the centuries, but male-rendered homilies always seemed both to Margaret Ingraham, my sometime writing partner, and me to fall short at times of being fully gendered. There is a fierceness in those women that somehow has often gotten too readily lost in that transposition.

Accordingly, she and I set out some time ago to write a suite of poems—or, if you will, a collection of performed monologues—intended to give voice, restored power, and even daring to some of our matriarchs. Those pieces, though far from complete as a set, are still accumulating; and while I shall not be able to further their number, Margaret, as the Poetess, pray God, will.

Meanwhile, in order to offer up some "sense" or aura of what we strive for, we begin here with the opening few lines of the first Canto in which two of the many who have come to sing in my own heart will speak their pieces. As the reader will, we hope, understand, the Voice of the Canto is Natalie Bartlum; the opening lament of Sarah is Ingraham and then, re-couched, my voice speaking as the Crone.

EXCERPTS FROM "THE MOTHERS OF THE FAITH"

Being a History in Three Books as Told by Three Voices:
The Principal Singer, a Poetess, and a Crone

⟨α⟩A Natalie Bartlum Poem

CANTO ONE

Listen, my daughters, to a song of redemption.
Give ear and give heart to all that we say.
We will sing of the past and the lessons we're given—
Long hallowed the stories and wonders we'll show.
We'll honor a Torah, which was and is ever,
And follow a road that as travelers we know. . .

Ours is an old psalm of praise and thanksgiving.
Ours is a new song we sing to the Living
And tell out the history for others not born.
Draw near and hear from the voices of women
Stories of longing, verses of song.
Follow beside us as we proclaim our delivering,
As we sing all the mysteries the mothers have known. . .

. . .The Poetess listens to hearts' secret yearnings
And learns ancient lessons she takes for her own:

> *"I want to be like Sarah*
> *Laughing myself*
> *Into a fervent faith*
> *That mocks my own denial*
> *Cracking the smile*
> *That breaks the yolk*
> *And sends the promise*
> *Streaming forth*
> *From barren womb*
> *To bless the generations."*. . .

. . .But listening alone and so intent
Perhaps only the aged Crone could see
That Sarah knew it to be a bitter vanity
To disown how utterly she failed,
And all alone she heard her sing out
The longing days of her travail:

> *My husband*
> *was always afraid*
> *of my beauty*
> *but I*
> *have used it well*
> *and childless*
> *I have sinned*
> *only once against a child*
> *because of his father's pride*
> *driving Ishmael off to die*
> *in which I failed*
> *the little bastard*
> *being fed instead*
> *by angel hands*
> *and now at peace*
> *in the safe house of my age*
> *I am made*
> *to bear*
> *a slave girl's pain*
> *because Abram and his angels*
> *need another son*
> *another puck*
> *in some cosmic game.*
> *Ha! and Ha! again*
> *I laugh*
> *because I am afraid*
> *the way of women*
> *is not done with me*
> *nor I with it*
> *not yet.*

. . .Now as she held to hope
It might have seemed in time
That age became supplanter of her dream
And yet so resolute was she
To stand against that chance
The Crone could hear Rebekah's song
As she withdrew each day to pray:

> *My father-in-law's blood*
> *runs strong in me,*
> *the pulse of God*
> *strumming through*
> *the beds of time.*
>
> *Of my husband*
> *time and history*
> *no doubt*
> *will say*
> *either nothing*
> *or not much.*
>
> *But were the matter*
> *in my hand,*
> *I would write him*
> *large,*
> *for he was,*
> *in all his ways,*
> *a man for me.*
>
> *He brought me*
> *Abraham's seed;*
> *and I winnowed*
> *what he brought*
> *until two possibilities*
> *fought in me:*

the gross, the hairy, the red
whom Isaac loved,
and the wily one,
that slick son
of time
out of whom
Yahweh and I
would make
the world.

Guiltless Ease

I would sing the horizontal man
Whose being spreads across his world
And ingests the whole of all it meets—
The man whose point of view
Can move with guiltless ease
Along the route of stimuli—
The man who spreads and is content
To wait upon infinity for the form
And holds his time as wisely spent
In purging evil from his mind—
A man who, in the exercise of taste,
Finds the joy of the earth
In being filter for the world.

The Re-Decorating

For Rose, to whom it happened

What does it mean
When a middle-aged man,
A scholar in Spanish and French,
Decides he must have
A bedroom that's new—
Fresh mattress and springs—
A headboard for two?

No more, I suspect,
Than it means
When his wife considers new sheets,
A pillow or two,
And, to stand watch by the bed,
A lamp that is blue.

What does it mean?
Not much, I suspect,
Except that she's through
And now they are free
To enjoy her sheets
(As well as his bed)
In ways they both knew,
But couldn't in youth.

So what I say is hurrah
For the middle-aged man,
The scholar in Spanish and French.
He once gave his life to his art,
But now has lived long
And is free to give both
To his middle-aged wife.

And that's what it means
When a middle-aged man,
A scholar in Spanish and French,
Decides with his wife
That they really must have
A bedroom that's new,
Fresh mattress and springs,
And to stand guard on it all,
A lamp that is blue.

A bit of humor, for we too often forget the very real and ribald and delightful side of mature and/or post-menopausal sexuality. Rose and I had a good time sharing this part of her experience, sometimes to the discomfort of her truly courtly husband.

FOR THE LITTLE ONES

I
A Winter Song

'Tis said by the old folks of a winter's night,
When the corn pops and the fire burns bright,
That the angels, warmed in Heaven's holy light,
Prune and pluck their wings to fly aright.
But only the young and the very old, they say,
Can truly know that the downy snow
Is made of angels' wings.

II
A Springtime Tale

The fairies danced last even
And drank of apple-scented tea.
They slid the moonbeams' silvered way
To use our lawn for their queenly play.
They plucked mimosa pods for drums
And used her puffs for fairy thrones,
Bent the onion tufts for seats,
And cried the dew on crocus cheeks.
Now sure 'tis good,
And our house most blessed
Because the little people's feet have pressed
Our lawn in such sweet caress.

Portrait

A friend of mine, age three,
An English child with curls,
Held up her cat to me—
"He's so dark to pet and very soft to see."
Fragrant summer child!
With just such words as these
I too believe
And pray your gentlest blessing
On the faith that dreams in me.

It always seemed to me to be the right of every writer's child to have something "just for us/me" from time to time, so I would post bits of verse occasionally ... taping them to a door, sticking them on a pillow. I suspect they delighted me more in their making than they did the children in their finding.

Young Together at Our House

They take the kittens,
Slipping the comfort of them
Into jackets and shirts and scarves,
Sidling as cat-like as they can,
Through the kitchen and toward their rooms,
Humming to hide the purring,
In their innocence never knowing,
It is coming
As much from them
As from the folds
Of their jackets, sleeves, and scarves.

We spent most of our married and child-rearing years on a small, family farm; and nothing on a small family farm is more central than cats: cats to keep the mice out of the feed, cats to chase the crows away, cats to hiss the invading snake into retreat. But cats have kittens, and kittens are not cats. They are the ultimate playmates and soul mates for country-reared children; and try as we might, we never as parents learned how to stop the constant flow of kittens being spirited surreptitiously through the house and into bedrooms as well as beds. I finally gave up; and one afternoon this became my posted declaration of surrender.

Mary in Church

A child working at her figures
Adds the logic of her years
To the order of the world's
And sums the total with the scrawls
Of her private lines and chords.
The delightful dreamings of a mind
That dawdles with another's symbols
Renders into peaceful pose
The face of one too young to fear
The aftermath of desecrated forms.

TWO

THE PLACES
OF OUR LIFE

Sam and I lived in Memphis from time to time during many of those twenty mid-twentieth-century years of growing unrest that led ultimately to the Memphis Garbage Strike and culminated in Dr. King's assassination. Those years of watching helplessly the city's slow march through despair and toward inexorable destruction would, I think, have been unbearable had it not been for the means to hear at least some of the pulsing of hope still coursing beneath the agony.

The War

While my country hesitates
Beneath their shuffling feet
The young go aimlessly across our land
And atop from childhood into age
In half of their appointed time.

The Song of Walthal

Being the Story of a Mid-century Memphis Neighborhood

Walthal sleeps in summerland
Suburban to the city's sweep.
Where once the varied grasses grew,
Now her whitened houses stand
And asphalt paves the arteries of man.
Built to hold the working crew
For a human wealth she never knew,
Walthal waits in sullen heat
For her time to be complete;
And waiting where she stood,
She sang the magnitude of man.

I heard the song of Walthal in the morning hour
And saw the dawn arise in a verdant shower;
Smelled the grasses in their mingled sweetness
And bethought me in the moment's fleetness
Of music played with stems for strings
And willows for an oboe's weeping.
All of Walthal, in quietness sleeping,
Sang of beauty, while in newness steeping.

I heard the song of Walthal in the troubled noon,
Heard the barren thunder clang the drums of doom;
Saw hot heat, in febrile stillness pressing,
Wet the walks in a sweaty tressing;
Watched the children dance the Congo's fevered beat
To the prism rhythms of a white-hot heat;
Saw love, like flowers, wilt away,
And beauty burned in the hellish May;
Sang of a land forever cursed,
Sang of Walthal always athirst.

I heard the song of Walthal ringing,
Down a dusty, treeless lane;
Heard the evening weep in sadness;
Heard the wind's upsurge of madness,
While all around in sacred orgy springing,
Wildly sang the priests of rain.
Men and women, in sorrow bending,
Human souls, like human twilights, ending,
Sang the song of Walthal in their rending.

The Hungry Spring

Avid amperes course along the wires
That cut across the acorn lakes.
Charges massed in awkward arcs
Cerebrate our loss of art.
Ambitions spur adamic man
(Alien name for the haunted damned)
And Southern anguish strides a canvas horse.

As It Should Be

In Mexico, the women sleep
Prostrate on the mountain tops
And peaks perform the functions
Of their better parts.

In the Times of Trouble

Human frames are not my kin
When they have not yet come to being men;
Still, I know and bear the pain
Of waiting without grief,
To catch the ache within my sterile heart
And lose this tension in my moral part.
'Til then, I'll go with God
And build with river dirt the age
When Less Than is the Devil's name;
When men like us work mouth to mouth
Each of all a feeling part
Without the law of feral codes;
When we all are sore
Because the labor pains of souls
Have kicked the body vaults of churls;
When out of blood and smoke and sin,
We all emerge as men.

Solstice, 1974

I lay awake on Solstice night
And heard decadent birds release
The first nocturnals of their year
In profligate paeans to those gods
That pagan men are quick to fear.
The sky was loud with city light;
The faded chords of motor sounds
Filled the measure of the song,
But crickets struck like metronomes;
And every bird made dissonance
Until the heated dawn
When, weary of their exorcism,
I met the sun with solipsism.

Autumn Rain

An urban peace has fallen in the rain
And stillness come in layers, washing down.
The world and I, while waiting here,
Were widowed in the death of sound.
But who of us who still have stayed
Can make from the silence of the rain
A eulogy upon the death of pain.

April in Lucy

The sleeping lassitude of Spring
That steals the purpose from my dreams
Never seems so sweet or good
As poets say it should.
The sensing of repose
In half-formed seeds and cores
Saps the luxury from ease
As across the sill of open pores
Slips the deceptiveness of Spring.

---

*Unlikely as it may sound, Lucy really is the name of a small farming and
railroad community in rural West Tennessee. Near Memphis, only twelve
miles directly east of the Mississippi, and with easy access to a connecting
Interstate system, Lucy became our "place" in the world. We farmed
the land and loved the village, rejoiced in the contradictions of its near-
proximity to the city and its total absorption in the ways, values, habits,
and personalities of nineteenth-century America. The poems that follow
here may never fully plumb the wonder or vitalism of that paradoxical
way of being, but they are my heart's truth as nearly as words can ever
capture and portray that shifting place of repose.*

Lucy at Dusk

Our pasture tonight
Is the warm teacups
My mother lifted from the water
And set to drain,
Their soapy bubbles blinking
On her hands
Like the fireflies
Across our meadow.

Ringnecks Return

A Natalie Bartlum Poem

You did not see the flock
masked by evening
drop from the sky
to the pond beyond the trees
but in the morning
found the geese
feeding in the stubbled fields
and counted them:
the same five birds miraculous
to land again
in so precise a resting place
bringing color to the solstice.

Two days, three nights this time
before the current changed,
signaled flight,
the tight formation
you plotted in your eye
to number them,
mounting to take the clouds
past all accounting
until they come again.

The Cranes

Where along their migratory way
These cranes may also stop
I can not say.
The river's a dozen miles from here,
But twice, sometimes more,
Each year
They drop,
A fleet of sails
On a sea
Of grass,
Like manna and the quails
Come from some other land
To say,
"This way! This way!"

View from the Bedroom Window

Like Harlequins of summer,
My fretful flowers,
Bloomless in the night,
Cast humid shadows
That come sniffing for the light.

A Sweet Sadness

A sky of surging butterflies
Cutting crosswise of the wind
Recalls for me those mountain years
When I, like them, would fly
Across the velvet thoughts
Of an Autumn afternoon.

THE "WOMAN AT MIDNIGHT" POEMS

I
Epiphany in Lucy

The sky is white again tonight,
A bowl of grace above the snow
That came in early afternoon.
I've walked our land these many years,
Good Bishop Seabury,
From cross to croft and back again,
The miles between the two
Shrinking with each year,
'Til now, in snow and midnight prayer,
Mother Church and Father God have come
To wed and blend
Into the simple light that lies
Frozen in glory
Along these limbs.

II
Lent in Lucy

We must think now,
In this time of winter.
We must stop
And we must consider—
What is this sleep
We fear to enter?

We must think now,
And we must consider
What it is
That we must consider,
While the wind sweeps
The gutters and the streets
Now in this time of winter.

When the mind sleeps,
The body withers and grows bitter.
We must stop now
And consider,
Before the lilies rise,
Why the god denies
An easy sleep.

We must stop now,
And we must consider
What it is that can be lost to us,
If the will should blanch and wither
Now
In this time of winter.

III
All Saints in Lucy

The marauding moonlight
Stalks the coyote
Across the pasture fields,
While miles away
The distant church bell
Tolls the Christian midnight.

It is the hour
Of most ancient prayer
When mothers everywhere
Seek to bind
The skirts of God
Around the beds
Of those who lie beside them,
Sleeping and unaware.

IV
Michaelmas in Lucy

These days
We waken into mornings
Still near to summer,
Still far from spring.
The first autumn weakness
Of the far-away sun
Fades the field
Where a herd of rocks
Sleeps ceaseless
In the crevices and rills
Of the broken meadow,
Warms its lichen skin,
Fills for the ancient earth
An emptiness in her mother-parts.
The chestnut trees around the pond,
Stripped down, gnarled and mean,
Bend with leanness
Like a senate of old men.
The restless wind,
Up from the western plain,
Bites the gutter and the tin
Loose along the roof line
Of the stolid barn.
Our bales whine,
Stroked by the violence
Of its discontent.
The withering pig-weeds,
Wilt and lie
Across the slender holes
Marauding ants have bored
Into the border clay.
The insect dead,
Killed by instincts of their own,
Are glue in the garden rot,

And glutted bees
Sink humless into trays
Inside the honey hive.
Yellow vetch and goldenrods
Send heavy pollen
As if it mattered
Into the air.
You and I turn back
In the silent afternoons,
Grateful for the promise
Of an early bed.
This vast shifting that still shapes us
Would also drive us mad,
Were it not for the long nights of knowing
A concern that lies beyond the reach
Of seasons.

All Hallows in Lucy

The fields of Lucy are thistle-filled,
Every mound
Between the barn lot and the pond
Is purple-crowned.
October's full-mooned yield
Leaves the pastures sticker-gowned
And sends the laughing children
Sweater-bound
Off in pumpkined coaches
To a corn-stalked school.

Midnight Services
Christmas Eve in Lucy

By lowered lights, the swirls in polished woods,
Or even more, the folds in priestly robes,
Make convolutions on a finished plane
And, for my drowsy eyes, a pleasant game.

Country Funeral in Lucy

Untouched and soul-eyed like sows they stand—
Two here, three at the door,
A cluster at the bier—
Then driven by a girdled dullness
They move to pat my friend
With stubby-fingered hands.
They cannot wait
To hang their crepe
On the newest of their sisterhood.

Summer Social at a Village Church

In the orchard
Where a herd of shadows
Is pasturing
Under the apple trees,
Women
As thin as empty houses
Are having tea.

The Bull Shooter

Above the smell of sweat
And the sound of god-damn,
He savors most the bellow of the calf
When, castrator in hand,
He grabs the balls
And bands them off.
His stoop-shouldered sons
(Who both call him Daddy)
Steer wide of him when he's in the lot,
Cowed as they are
By the bull and the god-damns.

Burglary

Almost a year now.
You've lost the face,
The years, the tastes
I thought you had
(sleuthed more from what you left
than what you took...
Why steal a coffee service and leave
a sheep-nosed clock?)
You were always,
from the first,
a quickened breath
when I, away from home,
wondered if you were breaking in.
You will always be
the carpet stain I walk around
and the bright gun I have bought.
As soon as you were no fun
to guess at anymore,
I learned to use it.
Someday I will shoot you
between the bedrooms and the kitchen door;
or I will write a poem
that leaves you bleeding there.
While the officers are reading,
I will explain you
were the one who
uninvited
climbed through the window into my mind;
that I loved my mother's silver teapot
and her wedding ring;
that every day this year
I've had to share with you;
and every branch against a screen,
every blue jay in the leaves,
every whining in the downspout,

has been your razor blade;
that today my car was in the shop
and that I have spent the entire afternoon
stunned
by how much younger you are
lying on the floor
than fading in my head.

---

*While some portraits of one's neighbors and fellow-parishioners are
just that—only portraits caught like snapshots in the affections of the
moment, some are not. I have included three such here. Burglary is
usually thought of as an urban crime—messy, reprehensible, furiously
impersonal. Not so in the small village where every one knows almost
every one else, including the heartache of "bad seed" or "mean kin" or
"troubles." We have been burglarized three times, each time knowing
the culprit, each time grieving with his embarrassed and grieving family.
Such intimacy of knowledge puts the burden of repair and redemption
on the whole village. I found, at least in my own case, that being able to
deflect anger into disposable, and sharable, words was a great balm. "The
Bull-Shooter," like all the other folk caught here, was very, very real and
a proximate neighbor. Only poetry proved strong enough to defuse him,
however; no prose would ever have been able to measure up to such a
chore. And as for Grandma, she too is real. Believe me. Grandpa knows.*

Sunday Lunch at Grandpa's

I

Every Sunday lunch,
Ramrod straight in too little space,
They sit around the kitchen table
Staring at the roast.
The children wiggle first,
Then grow silent as grown-up aunts.
Greed for meat and the succulence
Of country fruits
Pulls their lips and makes them thin,
As if afraid to move.
Looking down the corridor
Of plates and mouths
At his great, unweaned clan
Still sucking on her tits
Of applesauce and checkered cloth,
He wants her urgently,
Just as at every Sunday lunch,
Knows he could take her on the board
Of beans and cantaloupes and stares.
Instead, he cuts the roast,
Just as he does
At every Sunday lunch.

II

It amused her
Looking down the rows
At every Sunday lunch
To watch him pull against
The Johns and Beths and Joes
His haste begot for them—
Amuses her to play with him
In the public view of pears and three-year-olds.
Now that their young are grown,
She pipes the tune.
It amuses her
Every Sunday after lunch.

Tennessee is this country's "long state," stretching, like California turned sideways, for almost 550 miles from east to west. As a result, the state incorporates into itself three distinct geographies: the high, primitive, Celtic-infused mountains of the Blue Ridge and the Great Smokies and the Appalachian hill country; the mid-portion of rivers and commerce and meadows and good horse country and the music of Americana; and the deadly flat, hot, delta land that borders the Mississippi and grows the country's cotton and soybeans and blues and soul. These three distinct "countries" and cultures operate, sometimes very uneasily, under one government structure but with a palpable and almost uncanny pride on the part of each for its two sisters in the Tennessee triad.

Sam and I were born and reared in East Tennessee, in mountain country, our lives infused with Celtic sensibilities and mountain frugalities, rejoicing in a geography we did not know, until years later, was not the birthright of every American. Someone once said to me, "I can hear the mountains in everything you write," and I pray God that may be so. Certainly I have chosen to include here one or two pieces as examples of that.

The other or western end of Tennessee is "River" just as surely as the eastern end is "Mountain." My father was reared in West Tennessee, his home place being essentially on the River. He grew up, as did every West Tennessee boy of his generation, testing himself and his manliness against the River's constant caprices and delights. After Sam and I moved to West Tennessee, we found that our own sons—and to some extent our adventurous daughters—felt compelled to engage the Mississippi and the bodies like Reelfoot Lake that it formed as testing grounds for their own bravery and outdoor skills. Over the years, I too would sometimes leave Lucy and family to retreat with a writing project or deadline, always going to the little town of Tiptonville where I could rent a cabin for a song and then listen all day and all night to its cadences, the cadences of my blood and kin and heritage.

The Clouds

Promethean on the mountaintops,
Arms bent and legs apart,
A giant stood astride the universe
And yodeled to his mountain love.
She swept across the crumbling peaks,
A Titaness in gold and white,
To wrap her ancient skirts around his feet,
Until the failing of the sun
Had cast across the fields
The shadow of a single form,
Olympians in an act of love.

Mountain Songs

I

The instant is so bright and clear,
It belies the future fear
That the clutter of a wayward mind
May in time obscure
The beauty of this climb.

II

My joy wants a meadowsworth of song
To celebrate the sheep
Who feed along the rims
Of my native mountainscape.

Old Man River

My father called it
His boyhood's fiercest teacher,
And child-wise, I knew
He'd once used its even fury
As a mark to sound his own.
My mother turned from us
When he made river talk.
For her, its waters ran
With married tears.
And long before I'd aged enough
To want or rear a man,
She'd willed on me
The anger of her years.
There's a bridge above it now—
Tightly built—
No different from the land—
But it can no more bear my sons
Across his hunger
Than it can lift my breath
Above her fears.

Tiptonville, Tennessee

I've come home again,
Back to the earth that bore me,
To the silent land and the cypress lake,
Back to the family dead
Who always knew I'd come;
To the town my father owned.
I've come to buy it back
With my poetry and my pen—
O hungry land that holds my family dead.

Atlantis
The Isle of Palms

Where gulls on oceans drift
And water sculls a hanging clift,
The tide lays down its polished lore
Upon a timid, blushing shore
And writes in roundly runic script
The canons of earth's oldest crypt.

The bleaching beach of sand,
Girthing edge for a primal land,
Guards the thermal fusing bed
For the residue of fallen dead
Where heat and time alike demand
A resurrection far from man.

That neutral white of untracked beach,
Where swamps with flying oceans sleep,
When the lowered tide has come,
Is mirror for the dying sun,
While unfettered shadows creep
Into a lapping, silent deep.

Not only is Tennessee created of a strange, in some ways aberrant, geography, but so too is much of the South. Or more properly put, the South has retained a kind of primordial nakedness and, in places, near-animism that inform its progeny and form its mystique. No place better exemplified or captured or infused that untamed and holy wildness of disposition and presence than did the Isle of Palms in the years preceding the twenty-first century.

Located just off the coast of South Carolina, the Isle has been tamed now (save on certain days and in certain seasons when she still chooses to toss her angry mane at the world that would contain her) but the mystery of her will live always in my soul, and hopefully in my words, as it does in the hearts and words of many others.

Likewise, Thunderbolt Island—of which there are many, by the way, almost every state in the East and South finding in those words the power of the ancient gods—stands, in whatever state one engages it, as uncompromising testimony to what cannot be named, but must be known by the sheer force of its own will and the remembering imagination.

As for Hope, Arkansas, it too is a magical place. Like a ley line, it marks that singular meridian or stratum where Arkansas and the South abruptly and without apology become Texas and the West. Like stepping through a door, moving from one side of Hope to the other is to move into an entirely different cosmos. It is always a beautiful and sometimes an unsettling thing.

Thunderbolt Island

A Natalie Bartlum Poem

After the storm
straining the solstice,
it could have been
any two days' light
hanging behind the Spanish moss
where skydark water
circles the marsh grasses
like a tide the moon refuses
to take back.
The creek is a lost undertow
only the arched fish knows
to pull toward its mouth.
Black as live oak's shadow,
the tongues of water
are still surface legends,
As midnight edges from the marsh
an egret, lifting lightning, shrieks
to beckon flight wings will not follow
as if the call were enough;
earth slips her moorings
back into the night.

Hope, Arkansas

A Natalie Bartlum Poem

Near that town
barely two miles east
where the land
turns itself to Texas
before the line,
she gave herself to the ditch,
to the concave promise
of the half grave.
A small doe,
beige as the dust,
she left the cooling of her flesh
to the cooling earth
of the still, March dusk.
Impatient in leaving
her eyes open,
she forgot her stare
would summon the crow
to land and test the age of death,
to begin the ancient feast
that finally completes
the halfness of a ditch.

THREE

ARS POETICA

Poetry is the most self-conscious of the arts; and never was there a poet, or even a mediocre poetizer, who did not mourn without relief for the thing that could have been—should have been—would have been—had only the gift been greater or the practitioner purer or the moment more disciplined. The result, hiding around and about in almost every portfolio I have ever chanced to look into, is a cache or so of such regrets as these ... songs of the half-forgotten, memories of the still-restless dead.

Of Poetry

Say not to me
That genius, rent into its several parts,
May yet be mighty genius still,
And say not to me as well
That a child full dumb of mental ear
Can not naively hear
Or sweetly shed an untutored tear.
No, genius lies, and always has,
In perfect peace between just two
That the songs we naively hear
Become in time
The songs we share.

The Business of Versifying

Word and line—
The seen and heard—
Composition through design
Make us prophets of the time
When we at last will find
In children's chants
The purposes of rhyme.

So Fragile a Thing

Labored line
Grown weary out of time,
You dare to leave me now—
Musicless and free—
With just the ghosting rhyme
Of the image you had said
Would be.

Restless

The winter moon that delays
Too long above the edge
Of a weary morning sky
Is like the perfect phrase
That broods in dissonance
Because my mind cannot contrive
A context for its poetry.

Morning Lament

In their awakened morning life,
They limply lie – my lilting lines –
Too labored now to fly,
And loosely hold in languid grasp
The half-remembered chants
Of lyrics lost in melody.
The songs my dreaming poured
To fill the night of sleep
Have overflowed the vaulted domes
Of haunted, verbal forms;
But whispered by the phantom dead,
Those reverberating tones,
Rolling through the cavern depths within,
Still hear the notes impound
The morning ghosts of
Their dying sounds.

Brooks Memorial
Poet-In-Residence

The gallery has faded to dusty rose—
a pastel dying into gray;
yet even now a muted haze
still clings to the edge of every frame
like rolls of ginning fluff,
half-tinting all that's left
of sun and light and day,
as if the color and the form
from off the walls and floor
had been moving toward the door
when they chanced to die
along the window sills.

If this is indeed to be an autobiography of sorts, then it must include at least some small reference to the years between 1977 and 1987 when I served as Poet-In-Residence at the Memphis Brooks Museum of Art. Much of that work involved an "Artist-in-the-Schools" type of program in which the joy and the challenge lay in teaching children how to capture their lives and experience, their sorrows and their wonders in words—how to catch those gifts of growing up so lightly and so magically as to weave them forever into their lives. Children, given any kind of opportunity at all, are instinctively good at this; and more superb, if naïve, poetry came out of those years than could ever be catalogued now. And even all these many years later, I still recall with poignancy and clarity the many late afternoons when, our time together over and the children all gone back to their schools, I stood in the darkening gallery and rested a while among the sweet, gentle ghosts we had conjured there.

FOUR

ENUIGS

Enuigs (sometimes written as Enuegs) are a glorious, but now almost totally lost, part of the history and tradition of Western poetry. As any honest poet will tell you, we as a culture have become much too proper and politic for our own good over the last few centuries with our poetry and, in doing so, have denied ourselves, among other things, the marvelously curative practice of writing enuigs. That strange word means, in polite form, vexatious or vexations. In the street language from which it comes, however, it means something much closer to a holy and acerbic bitch; and for centuries, it allowed poets to both vent their spleen and also complain therapeutically about the follies of life.

I can honestly say that I have mourned the passing of enuigs more than that of almost any other ancient form of poetry and, given that circumstance, could not forgo including some here. The tone is not always gentle, nor the sentiments always laudable, but they are at least honest. Thus, like Catullus from Roman literature, I upon occasion have just simply had too much of poetry-worship and poet-idolatry; and thus I joined him years ago in looking askance at some of what even accomplished poets can do when, as a group, we become too impressed with ourselves. Likewise, as a professional religionist and sometime academic, I have often found relief in using enuigs to vent my irritation at too much theologizing and too much cerebrating.

In the Company of Poets

After the Manner of Catullus

Like Aleph, the sacred cow,
Festooned with garlands of blooms,
Poetry has carried us all our life
On her warm back
Toward Xanadu,
Leaving behind us there
A waft of strong air
And even an exquisite turd or two.

A Somewhat Sardonic Corrective

(with apologies, of course)

Petros, that jolly old bonhoffer,
Sitting haunched beside the sea,
Never knew that I and Thou
Would contemplate so existentially
The Cost of Mass Discipleship.
But then, poor buber, he never knew
That Van Buren would become
A major U.S. precedent.
In the hallowed towns of Galilee,
Only low-born farmers tilliched,
And even the shackled galley slaves
Could scarce be seen to niebur.
Poor old Petros, sitting on that rock,
Watched a sea on which he'd walked
And never dreamed of distant things
So marvelous or so ecumenical.

Of Theologians

Say not to me
That learned men,
Grown sere and brown,
Add aught to music
By dissecting it to sound.

Yet Another Professional Meeting

Tobacco smoke that clings
Against the windowed wall
To form a film upon
The dark, obstructing glass
Suspends itself in brown
Above the crowd of men
And seems to make a halo
For the after-dinner sin
Of wisdom watered down
By weariness and gin.

On Study

Chameleon of the soul I go
From thought to thought
As ideas flow like tides
Within the sea of me,
And find myself displeased to know
That never with two different men
Can I stand and hold
The constancy of me.

Bathroom Chores
A Ditty

Water lines in dark commodes
And dirty rings in bathtub drains,
Spotted Grecoes on my polished pipe...
These, my boy, are the parts of you
I'll gladly give a wife.

---

*And last, just for fun, enuigs (which I often labeled as "ditties") got
posted at our house from time to time as maternal commentary. This one,
posted years ago on the wall of a teen-aged son's bathroom, pretty much
covers the possibilities of the genre.*

FIVE

COMMEMORATIVE

In the course of every writer's life, if he or she is fortunate, there will come an opportunity or two to use one's craft to celebrate another human being or a singular human event ... to express gratitude ... to remark, for the sheer joy of it, upon the truly remarkable in this, our shared business of being human. I have chosen four such folk and events to include here.

⟵

It would be hard now to conjure, for our more sophisticated and informed astrophysical times, the impact in 1973 of the sighting of a new comet, Kohoutek. It seemed almost as though the whole of history were waiting to see this thing whose like had never come our way before. Popular music was written about it, plays built around it. It was to be the first comet we would be able to see from a manned space craft, the first time this creature that was another world had entered into our solar system. The hype was ubiquitous and contagious. It was also destined to never be fully realized, for 1973 was a singularly cloud-obstructed year in which the rains simply would not fall. Next door to us, however, was a most ancient and wise and faithful man. Claude A. Titsche was an Orthodox Jew who, in the course of our years of shared neighboring, instructed us by example more about Judaism and the life of wide-eyed, realistic faith than anyone else ever was to do. Each day, he would go out onto his porch in the twilight, scan the sky for what still was not visible, smile, and go back in to wait for another day. Kohoutek would come.

And finally it did. It broke through the mists and clouds of earth's mantle in late December, but Mr. Titsche had already slipped away by then. What he had left behind, instead, however, was faith ... pure naked faith that never waivered; and his truth has informed every one of us in all the years since we watched the Jew, who watched the sky for the rains that hesitated so long that year. God rest his soul.

The Comet Kohoutek, 1973

In memory of a neighbor who died that year

So long that year, so long
Before the winter came.
The sky hung low, heavy with snow
And with the rains that would not come
That year.
Next door the ancient Jew was cold
With an old man's cold,
His face as gray as the light
He watched in
Waiting for Kohoutek.

Part of history,
Part of time,
Part of all mankind,
I watched the Jew
Who watched the sky
To find the sign
That hid behind
Rains that would not come
That year.

Robert Hollabaugh, M.D.

Death laughed to see my son.
He was just passed three and pale—
So pale Death laughed to see.
Every day the fever rose
And the swelling of his neck,
And every day, the surgeon said, "Not yet."

He was just passed three
And Death laughed to see how thin he was
When they said, "This afternoon!"
And I said, "Oh, please, not yet!"

But because the surgeon said, "I'll play
At being God with God's permission,"
They took him anyway, so small and white.
I was alone, and Death laughed to see how pale,
Until God called from Surgery to say, "Not yet."

He's just passed four, my son,
And Life laughs to see how rosy-cheeked and fair.
But when he's come to age, I'm pledged
He'll learn the skills it takes
For God to call and say, "No, not yet."

---

*While the circumstances here are self-evident, no poem or essay or paean
could ever capture, even superficially, the gratitude and amazement out
of which this piece rose. While spontaneously written as a mother's
gifting to the healing surgeon, the piece has gone on to become a part of
Physician Appreciation observations as well.*

Ordinary Song

⟨⟩ A Natalie Bartlum Poem

I sing of the mountains that sing in me
the cadences of plaintive earth
and only give you back the land
that framed the valley of my birth.

I fed each day on mountain thyme
and nightly cradled with the quail.
I woke to walls of laurel leaf
and raised a morning song to hail
the line of sheep who grazed
across the valley rim.

I learned by heart the ancient sounds
of bird and pine, of stream and fawn,
waiting to hear spring waters clear
below the stones they played upon,
the litany of earth.

I sing of the mountains that sing in me
soft harmonies I've known from birth.
I only give you back the land again
and the plain magnificence of earth.

This, as the sub-head indicates, is a Natalie Bartlum Poem. Originally, it was simply a piece in which, by working together, the two of us were trying to capture and celebrate our mutual love of the mountain and hill country of Tennessee. Much to our delight, as well as surprise, the piece somehow jumped the confines of those far simpler intentions and the first and last stanzas are now inscribed permanently in the wall of the Bicentennial Capitol Mall in Nashville.

American Genesis

In Memory of My Mother-In-Law

On Ash Wednesday we said,
"Let's go home again—
A few days, a week,
Spend a while—
We'll tell no one."
So we left
And ate fish across the state
On our way home again.

(Do you remember—
It was always I who said,
"You can't go home again?")

It was night and cold
And the first Sunday into Lent
When we knocked on your door
And the old woman who had been your mother,
The gnome who kept the place,
Brought her mastiff on its chain
Before she unlatched the door
And we went in, as if we were home again.

The house was quiet,
Clean as the mountains
And twice as old as home had been.
But we slept on the folded-down cot
That still served her as a front-room couch,
Coming together in the middle
Where the springs collected us
And in the morning staying there,
Content to be ourselves.
She said she wanted to go home again
And you said you'd take her there;
What she meant was a graveyard and some stones,

A rolling tract and the broken trees
Back in the fields that bred her.
We took her in the lemon sun
And the warming Lenten air,
Back to stand and dream:

Nannie Porter Lowe
September 26, 1861
August 5, 1891
Lloyd Lee Lowe
August 5, 1891
November 3, 1891

O, God, I could not bear to see her there!
I could not watch her move her lips
While she went home again.

Once her house, but now a barn
Where she had lived when she was young—
Where she had taken you when she went home.
Now the hay was stored in every room
And shoved against each door.
But her flowers were still in front,
And her uncle's holly tree,
And the spring,
And the little hills across the way
Where her mother first had grown—
Where she had gone when she went home.

So we left the house and graves
And drove her out along the roads
That wound around the hills
Until we came to places she had known
Because her mother had once been young,
Because her mother's mother once had called them home.
And you could scarcely bear the pain, I could tell,
Of watching her come here again
To see her mother's home.

Fish are never sold on country roads
Where steeples grow,
So we brought her back to town
And left her with her dog
While we ate our fill
And went to roam the hills.

(What was it I had wanted here
When I had asked if you would bring me home?)

You walked out among the hills
Until we found the place
Where the valley cuts around the lake
And the trail of fading blazes marks the way
The timberjacks and Clinchfield men used to walk
When we were children in the town
And they would come down for Eastertime
To trudge home again.

We drank from Jones's Branch
And crossed its rocky fords
Until at last we were caught
By the gentle cloth of mountain dark
In some greening mountain gap.

We made camp and in the lantern light
Fashioned walking sticks
From the birches you had hacked.
And their whiteness—limber, smooth, and wet—
Was like your house that night
When I first began to guess
That you were home again.

We broke camp and walked again
Across the Unaka's crests,
Lean and thin,
And breathed the air that fed us
When we were young and knew

That the woods, the laurels and the pines,
Were always there.

We chewed the deer moss
And watched the galax growing greener
As we climbed.
Until you said,
"There's snow ahead."

At first I did not see it—
It had been so long,
So many years I had not smelled it.
It fell, deep-white flakes of cold,
But we were warm, for it was Eastertime,
And we walked the hills
Until at last the blazes grew too dim,
Lost in the silvered light,
And the ice was going hard around us.

So we came out again,
Down the grade and into some tiny mountain town
Where we hailed a car
And paid the man
To haul us home again.

The ancient one smiled and cooked
And stirred her pots
And fed her dog,
Happy to have us back again.

(How long had it been?
How long that we'd been gone?)

The acres where our children played
When we used to bring them home
And where your father's garden grew—
All grown now to Interstate,
And who could ever know

How much I'd miss the vining peas
And the swelling shocks of corn,
The grafting of an apple branch?

But there's no grief in the ageless one—
She's as flexible as time
And twice as free—
Because this was never really home,
Just the place they settled in
When they came to town
With some flowers, a wagon, and a tree.

We left her with her thoughts,
Lost among her pots,
And found our way to church.
The priest had stopped the mass to preach.

He said there was some rite—
(Was it baptism? The Eucharist? or both?)
That there was some rite by which
We all come home.

But then he said no more,
And we left the loaf and wine,
For it was almost Eastertime,
And we drove again
'Til we came at last to our own door,
And the children who were waiting there said,
"Oh, you've come home again,"

But they never asked why we went.
And their children, toddling down the drive
To grab and hug at you,
Only cared
That we were home for Eastertime.

Recognized by the American Revolution Bicentennial of Tennessee as a Bicentennial Poem for Tennessee.

Chet

We laid aside the last today
Of a self-afflicted life—
A boy who in suicide
Was kinder to his mother
Than to us.

SIX

ENDINGS

All Celibacy Laid Aside

This harp on which I used to play, dear,
No longer hums beneath my touch;
As if, although I still own the harp,
You only own the tune.
That pipe on which I know you've played
Is mine alone to blow,
As if, although you own the horn,
'Tis now I who own the tune.

To Sappho

A female specter sat and sang
A vicious lullaby. The lyre
Against her tuniced chest
Made peaceful chords between her violent words;
The song that raged across the space
Between her ghost and me
Tore with avarice at my thoughts.

So wildly did she chant,
So calmly did she strum,
That her semblance and her sound
Must have maddened me;
For I answered, across that room,
With a frenzy that I knew
Was pagan as her tune.

She who had risen from Atlantis
Had sung with lustfulness of men
Erect in passions and in form,
But I who sat upon a cushioned chair
Could reason no retort
I heard my voice filling stanzas
With the visions of Another's plan:

"I have sung the seasons—
No man ever more—
And pulled my skin from off my bones
To find if I am growing thin.
I have lain in open space
And bathed my hair in sun
But I can no longer.

"Make a canticle for sheep
Or a eucharist from thyme.
Our seasons sink into their ending.

The body dies with their demise.
I have read the records of my kin
And at their burial I will know the litany,
For I would be interred a suicide with men."

If she had sung a lullaby of madness
To embryos before their time,
Then I had surely spoken history
To those whose creation only waited
For the death of form.
Not content, my words began a mystery
Addressed to them who were to be:

Do not ponder over us
Or play at Yorick with our heads.
We go laughingly
Rolling in the stubbled grass;
Was always health for us,
And grass is what we wish to be
Beneath the walls of Babylon.

"You took the earth in Ragnarok—
God knows she was soul to us—
We never knew the formulae
And space ran out on us.
There was no room (or not enough)
And, built to fill up area,
We turned to holocaust.

"Lovely as you are
You are more alien than she,
But essence of our dust
From the ashes of my fire
Where I in embers lie
Remembered and aware
I see you rising now."

Those beings seemed to float and generate,
To rend and then recongregate
I yearned to move closer;
But held within the barriers of time,
Within a space that I had loved
Before the specter form had come
I knew at last the truth of comedy.

She and I we fastened to the ground
Like the gateposts of an era
That ran between us to no end.
Then the ghost and I clasped hands
And lying down together
I drifted into union
And heard a distant chorus say:

"Lay aside the flesh" was too divine—
And so we killed each other,
Each man signing manumission
For his world-bound brother.
Near the end we lived within our heads
But skulls are hard as bone
Until we bashed them in.

The weak who had no guts for giving up
Sought for some adjusted aims
And them we fed on the carrion of dreams,
While we who knew and saw
Pinched our flesh and found,
At each progressive gauge,
That we were grown more thin.

"We lived our roles too morally
And posturings used up all our time
But in copulation we could feel
That we were still alive.
We heard our music with our trunks
And so exercised our eyes with vertigo
That we did not recognize the fire."

Rousing from the troubled lull of dreams
I saw the specter dressing in my clothes
And the image that was me made benediction:
"I love you, vapors of myself
Ethereal and unchained;
But I have also loved
The saltiness of blood."

It is only in our dying
That the last of any sound
Flows sweet as lyric poetry
Running from a Sappho down;
For she sang for us,
As we now sing for you,
A lullaby for embryos.

Wisdom

Everyone assumes
That the perfumes
Of August
Are the work of springtime's buds
Aging into blooms.
But the fading rose,
In her dying, knows,
It is the joy of ceasing
That distills perfume.

The Hiatus

There is a time within the season of our years
When the earth rests beneath our weight
Silent as a sparrow in the snow,
And we hesitate upon the brink
Of an exquisite indecision.

Aubade

A Natalie Bartlum Poem

Every morning early
before the wrens,
the elderly rise and go
places no one knows of.
Cheekbones red with rouge,
sensing if they walked
too plainly into life,
out and in,
their boldness would offend.
And so they go,
frail fingers, fragile skin
warmed in the secret wind
they follow,
rising on a breath
thin enough to flit and bend
and turn, victorious
in the end,
to light
beyond the places
of the wren.

Old Woman

He brought her flowers –
Roses and fern and lilac bloom.
"A single bud would do,"
But she smiled and took the huge bouquet
Up into their room.

He brought her mums from the garden,
Marigolds from between the rows,
Gladiolas in their season,
Squash blooms in the fall.
She took them all,
But what she wanted was
A single bloom.

They grew brown like the apples
In their ageing orchard.
When the flowers died,
He brought her thyme
And chives and radish clumps.
She smiled and waited for her rose.

Their world grew small again.
He sold the herd and let the barn,
But she smiled when,
By the kitchen door,
He set a single rose to bloom.

She takes it now,
As bud by bud,
Across the fields and through the fence
She goes
To lay upon his grave
One single bloom.

Remembrance in Maturity

Adrift in the not quite night,
At the end of a too-still day,
I heard a whistler whistle a tune
Which was as faint and fair
As the cat-gray air
Of that far-away time
In the dawn of my sixtieth year
When I watched as the distant clouds
Begin to fold
Their seductive pinks away.

In Memoriam

Beautiful I would have you,
But not quite perfect,
Lest there be no place
By which to grasp you now
With a love that finds
The wrinkles of imperfection
Sweeter to the lips and tongue
Than was the blandness
Of unscarred skin.

The Wake

When we were young,
The children small,
My fingers felt along
The fringes of their face.
My palms went flat at birth
To learn the curvings
Of their chests.

There are bonds that seal by hand.

So I dress you now,
Smooth your hair,
Close your lids,
And they must understand.

There are bonds that seal by hand.

The Campanile

Who hears these bells
Hears me.
Their bongs and trills
Are matters
Of a lifetime,
Not in their sounds,
But in my knowing
That who hears these bells
Hears me.

Manual Labor

The dust of Eden lay
New and dumb
Beneath the hands
That shaped it into man.

Who sleeps in me
And dreams these dreams
I can not see;
The womb is set
Too deep in me.

But fallen and aware
I at least can know
Whose hands it is are working there.

On Leaving

Self dies away,
The shell from around the life.
Like the chick from its egg,
What is, comes out,
And I am left,
Beak-bruised and broken,
While what was becoming
All these years
Waddles, still half-stunned,
Towards the light.

INDEX TO THE POEMS

THE PHYLLIS A. TICKLE AWARD IN POETRY honors our longtime friend, advisor, and member of Paraclete Press's editorial board. This award will be given every other year, starting in 2016, to a poet unpublished in volume form. The award will provide for the publication, by Paraclete Poetry, of their first book of poems.

For many years, Phyllis helped guide and shape Paraclete Poetry. She recently wrote, "Paraclete is firmly rooted in presenting and curating religious poetry as that part of the verbal experience which, being couched more deeply in the aesthetic than the didactic, has deep resonance and potent significance for the shaping of the surrounding culture."

Book proposals of poems and other supporting materials may be emailed as a single file to Mark S. Burrows, Series Editor, Paraclete Poetry, at this address: markburrows@paracletepress.com.

To make a contribution to The Phyllis A. Tickle Award in Poetry, please send a check made payable to:

THE PHYLLIS A. TICKLE AWARD IN POETRY FUND
c/o Paraclete Press
PO Box 1568
Orleans, MA 02653

ABOUT PARACLETE PRESS

WHO WE ARE

Paraclete Press is a publisher of books, recordings, and DVDs on Christian spirituality. Our publishing represents a full expression of Christian belief and practice—from Catholic to Evangelical, from Protestant to Orthodox.

We are the publishing arm of the Community of Jesus, an ecumenical monastic community in the Benedictine tradition. As such, we are uniquely positioned in the marketplace without connection to a large corporation and with informal relationships to many branches and denominations of faith.

WHAT WE ARE DOING

PARACLETE PRESS BOOKS

Paraclete publishes books that show the richness and depth of what it means to be Christian. Although Benedictine spirituality is at the heart of all that we do, we publish books that reflect the Christian experience across many cultures, time periods, and houses of worship. We publish books that nourish the vibrant life of the church and its people.

We have several different series, including the best-selling Paraclete Essentials and Paraclete Giants series of classic texts in contemporary English; Voices from the Monastery—men and women monastics writing about living a spiritual life today; award-winning poetry; best-selling gift books for children on the occasions of baptism and first communion; and the Active Prayer Series that brings creativity and liveliness to any life of prayer.

MOUNT TABOR BOOKS

Paraclete's newest series, Mount Tabor Books, focuses on liturgical worship, art and art history, ecumenism, and the first millennium church, and was created in conjunction with the Mount Tabor Ecumenical Centre for Art and Spirituality in Barga, Italy.

PARACLETE RECORDINGS

From Gregorian chant to contemporary American choral works, our recordings celebrate the best of sacred choral music composed through the centuries that create a space for heaven and earth to intersect. Paraclete Recordings is the record label representing the internationally acclaimed choir Gloriæ Dei Cantores, praised for their "rapt and fathomless spiritual intensity" by *American Record Guide*; the Gloriæ Dei Cantores Schola, specializing in the study and performance of Gregorian chant; and the other instrumental artists of the Gloriæ Dei Artes Foundation.

Paraclete Press is also privileged to be the exclusive North American distributor of the recordings of the Monastic Choir of St. Peter's Abbey in Solesmes, France, long considered to be a leading authority on Gregorian chant.

PARACLETE VIDEO

Our DVDs offer spiritual help, healing, and biblical guidance for a broad range of life issues including grief and loss, marriage, forgiveness, facing death, bullying, addictions, Alzheimer's, and spiritual formation.

LEARN MORE ABOUT US AT OUR WEBSITE:

WWW.PARACLETEPRESS.COM

OR PHONE US TOLL-FREE AT 1.800.451.5006

SCAN
TO
READ
MORE

MORE PARACLETE POETRY

99 Psalms

SAID

Translated by Mark S. Burrows

ISBN: 978-1-61261-294-2, $17.99, Paperback

These are poems of praise and lament, of questioning and wondering. In the tradition of the Hebrew psalmist, they find their voice in exile, in this case one that is both existential and geographical.

Slow Pilgrim

The Collected Poems of Scott Cairns

SCOTT CAIRNS

ISBN: 978-1-61261-657-5, $39.00, French flap paperback

"Among American poets of religious belief at the present time, none is more skillful, authentic, or convincing than Scott Cairns."

—B. H. FAIRCHILD, poet, National Book Critics Circle Award winner